**JB** JOSSEY-BASS™
A Wiley Brand

# Challenge Gifts and Grants

## 76 Ways to Multiply Your Fundraising Dollars

### Scott C. Stevenson, Editor

WILEY

978-1-118-69187-8   ISBN

978-1-118-70385-4   ISBN (online)

# Challenge Gifts and Grants

## 76 Ways to Multiply Your Fundraising Dollars

Published by

**Stevenson, Inc.**
P.O. Box 4528 • Sioux City, Iowa • 51104
Phone 712.239.3010 • Fax 712.239.2166

www.stevensoninc.com

## TABLE OF CONTENTS

## TABLE OF CONTENTS

## Challenge Gifts and Grants

## 76 Ways to Multiply Your Fundraising Dollars

### 1. Setting Up a Challenge Gift

A challenge gift can be a creative way to get one of your top donors to make a stretch gift to your campaign. But for such a gift to be effective, make sure the challenge is tied to increasing gifts from a group with which the donor has an affinity, says Lisa E. Grider, executive vice president and chief operating officer, Graham-Pelton Consulting Inc., (New York, NY).

During feasibility studies or casual conversations, Grider says, donors may communicate a particular strategy they would like your organization to pursue, such as increasing the number of new donors or getting more board members to give. That information can be used to encourage them to make a challenge gift.

When asking for a challenge gift, you are really asking for a second or stretch gift, says Grider: "Don't make the entire gift contingent on the challenge. The challenge piece should be an add-on; an additional gift beyond what they were considering."

Emphasize how the challenge gift will fulfill the donor's wish (e.g., increase number of new donors, encourage more board members to make gifts, etc.), she says: "For example, if a donor has told you that they see themselves making a gift of $500,000, but you know that because of their capacity they can make a larger gift, and because of conversations you have had with them, particularly during the feasibility study, that they are interested in seeing more new donors to the campaign, you could ask them to give an additional $500,000 as a match to all new donors. Your approach could be: 'Mr. Smith, you said that you wanted to see this board make a larger gift. We have a solution and need your help. What if we do X, Y, Z?'"

The type of challenge you set up — be it new/increased gifts, or gifts from certain groups such as board members or parents — should be driven by what you think would appeal to the challenge donor, Grider says. "For example, if your challenge donor is a parent, you would want to ask the donor to make a challenge to other parents."

*Source: Lisa E. Grider, Executive Vice President/COO, Graham-Pelton Consulting, Inc., New York, NY. Phone (908) 608-1388. E-mail: lgrider@grahampelton.com*

*Structuring a challenge as an addition to an outright gift increases the overall donation and guarantees a minimum level of support.*

### 2. Midyear Challenge Brings New Life to Lagging Gift Support

It's pretty common for annual fund efforts to lose momentum somewhere by the end of the second and third quarter. Current donors have either made their gifts or pledged to make a gift by year-end and new prospects have been approached and either will or won't make a gift before the fiscal year ends. Now what?

That's where a midyear challenge gift can bring new life to your annual giving effort. Whether the challenge matches all new and increased gifts, all gifts in excess of a certain amount or some other criteria, a challenge provides a great publicity tool that refocuses attention on the importance of meeting or exceeding your goal by year-end. Additionally, a midyear challenge tends to reinvigorate those — both staff and volunteers alike — who are doing the asking.

Rather than scrambling to find a donor willing to issue a challenge at the last minute, begin identifying and contacting potential challenge donors as you get your fiscal year under way.

# 3. Ideas to Work Smarter in Today's Economy

To meet or even surpass this year's fundraising goals — perhaps with a smaller operating budget — requires more focused effort. To work smarter in today's economy:

1. **Make donor retention the top priority**, especially those who give at higher levels. It's much more time- and cost-effective to retain past donors than to find new ones.

2. **Direct fundraising efforts toward higher-end donors.** If your top annual giving club includes donors at the $1,000-and-above level, for instance, develop several strategies aimed at that level of giving. Why go after 10 $100 gifts when it takes no more effort to go after 10 $1,000 gifts?

3. **Work at securing a challenge gift.** Challenge gifts provide two sources of gifts: the donor who makes the challenge and everyone who matches it.

4. **Get board members and volunteers more actively engaged.** Convince loyal supporters about the urgency of meeting this year's goal, and ask them to get involved with your fund development efforts in very specific ways.

5. **Drop past efforts that yielded marginal returns.** It's easy to keep doing what's been done in the past because "we've always done it that way." Evaluate past efforts and be willing to discontinue what didn't produce in the past.

*Not sure if the time is right to discontinue a long-time event? Seek the opinions of top supporters and donors.*

# 4. Appeal to Ego-driven Donors

Persons who enjoy being at the forefront of attention may require a different solicitation approach. To help bring about a major gift from someone who relishes public attention while bringing in new revenue, host an "in-honor" dinner or roast. Use these steps to craft an event that best suits your organization:

1. **Use the promise of a captive audience to close the gift.** After continued cultivation, approach your major gift prospect to suggest he/she be the guest of honor at a dinner hosted by your organization to announce his/her major gift. The pull of public limelight may be just what it takes for the person to agree to your ask. The donor may even choose to cover event costs.

2. **Make it a challenge gift.** The donor will be even more thrilled with the publicity that goes with a gift that encourages others to give as well, and a challenge gift will extend the period of recognition for the major donor.

3. **Make it difficult to say "no."** Take responsibility for coordinating the dinner so the donor's sole duty is to help with the guest list and show up.

4. **Arrange a program that directs attention to the donor.** Whether you arrange for individuals to step forward and make positive comments about the donor or the donor agrees to a roast format, the honoree will be the center of attention for the evening.

5. **Announce the gift.** Use the announcement of the donor's gift and challenge as a climax of the evening's festivities.

While this method itself may not produce a major gift, it will certainly add a strong incentive for persons who thrive on public recognition.

*Offer recognition to those who relish it, but remember that putting one person in the spotlight too often can alienate other major donors.*

## 5. Timely Challenge Encourages New Donations

Creating loyalty in young donors can lead to bigger payoffs in the future.

Knowing this, Jamie Stack Leszczynski, associate director of annual giving, The Fund for Oswego (Oswego, NY), and development staff created a 10-year reunion challenge to not only celebrate alumni anniversaries, but also engage them as donors.

Leszczynski secures volunteers from the class preparing to celebrate its 10-year reunion to serve as chairs of the challenge, help create a goal and solicit classmates.

Classmates receive two mail solicitations challenging them to make a donation to help reach the goal in honor of their 10th reunion year. Volunteers also send e-mails and make phone calls to classmates.

The goal for the graduating class of 1998 was $10,000, playing off the 10-year reunion. By the end of the fiscal year, the school had secured 58 new donors, approximately 4 percent of the class, and raised $7,869. Matching gifts and pledge payments helped them reach their goal.

Class of 1999 volunteers challenged fellow graduates to not only reach the bar of giving $10,000, but to raise it. A letter to class members (shown at left) noted that if each class member gave just $19.99 they could raise $28,585.

Other changes to the Class of 1999 campaign included creation of a class website (e.g., "You know you attended Oswego from 1995-1999 when you remember…") and Facebook page, she says, noting: "We realized after the class of 1998 that if you focus on the 10-year class and give them a little more attention, the campaign will be successful."

She says this year's challenge is also focusing more on participation, with the hope that this push will re-engage those students who have lost contact. "Hopefully this will engage alumni who have not donated in the past, connecting them with the campus once again."

Content not available in this edition

*This letter is one of several pieces 10-year reunion members received encouraging them to support an all-class fundraising effort for SUNY Oswego.*

*Source: Jamie Stack Leszczynski, Associate Director of Annual Giving, The Fund for Oswego, SUNY Oswego, Oswego, NY. Phone (315) 312-3121. E-mail: leszczyn@oswego.edu*

# 6. Partner With an Image-hungry Business

Consider forming a mutually beneficial alliance with businesses in your community that could stand to improve their images or gain a reputation for philanthropy.

Meet with officials of these businesses to explore project possibilities that enhance their public image and raise funds for your nonprofit. Your proposal of possibilities might include:

- A special fundraising event sponsored and staffed by the business.
- Use of their facilities and/or services by your organization.
- A public pledge that the business intends to donate a specific amount of employee time toward volunteer efforts with your organization.
- A commitment to underwrite start-up costs of a new program.

Be sure that your proposal includes tangible benefits geared toward the business being approached: number of news releases, television and radio opportunities, sponsorship signage, incentives for employee participation and more.

# 7. Know What a Challenge Gift Should Accomplish

When seeking to establish a challenge gift — a major gift given to a charity providing it is matched by gifts given by others — how much thought goes into what you want it to accomplish?

Naturally, the challenge gift itself is a major achievement, but how you use that gift to leverage other gifts represents an important part of any challenge.

Do you want to use the challenge to generate new, first-time gifts? Do you want to use it as a way to encourage increased giving? Perhaps you are interested in generating more gifts at, say, the $1,000-plus level.

Before approaching a would-be donor for a major challenge gift, know what it is you want that challenge to accomplish.

Here are some ways you can use a challenge gift to leverage others' giving:

*Try to find overlap between challenge donors' areas of interest and your organization's needs.*

✓ A general challenge that matches all gifts over a specified period of time. A challenge that matches any gift oftentimes has a ceiling: "The Turner Foundation will match any gift throughout the current fiscal year up to $1,000 per donor."

✓ One that matches donors who join a gift/membership club at a particular level during the course of the year.

✓ A challenge aimed at a particular group — recent graduates, those residing in a particular city or state, members of a particular profession.

✓ Those who have given first-time gifts and are being invited to give for a second year.

✓ Challenges directed to current and/or former board members.

✓ Those directed to employees — based on gift amount and/or percentage of employee participation.

✓ Multi-year challenges that encourage donors to also make a long-term commitment.

## 8. Challenge Gift Approaches

To motivate donors to match a challenger's gift over a multiyear period, convince the challenger to up the stakes in years two and three (and possibly beyond). For example, in year one the challenger will match anyone's gift on a 1:1 basis. In year two the challenger matches any gifts on a 2:1 basis, and in year three the match ratio jumps to 3:1.

## 9. What It Takes to Land a 'Kresge Challenge'

In 2008, Florida Southern College (Lakeland, FL) received a $600,000 Kresge Foundation Capital Challenge Grant to help with the construction of a new academic building for the study of literature and languages.

The challenge grant was also given to encourage broad-based participation from the college's alumni and friends. The terms of the grant required the college to raise the project balance of $1.97 million within 18 months.

"We met our goal five months ahead of schedule," says Lee Mayhall, vice president for college relations.

Securing a Kresge Foundation Challenge Grant is a lengthy process, she says, and requires a major commitment on the part of the institution's leadership: "Every one of our trustees made a financial commitment to the project prior to the submission of our proposal, with the president, trustees and volunteers participating in gift solicitations."

Prior to submission of their proposal, the college's president visited the foundation to discuss their challenge grant campaign strategy, she says.

A strong campaign was also important to the success of the proposal, says Mayhall: "The foundation assumes your project is worthy — they want to see a solid plan for achieving the balance of the project goal."

The college's plan included communications to stakeholders and staff, and volunteer involvement in the solicitation of top prospects (e.g., trustees, corporations and foundations, and individuals). "It also included a well-organized program of soliciting broad-based support from alumni, parents and faculty/staff," she says.

Once funded, it is crucial to stay in regular communication with your grants compliance officer, who wants your project to succeed, says Mayhall. The Kresge Foundation required periodic financial and construction progress reports.

She shares this advice for other fundraisers seeking to land a Kresge Challenge:

- Make sure that your project and fundraising timetable fit the foundation's guidelines. Ensure institutional commitment from the president, trustees, major gifts and annual fund staff, and your vice president for facilities. Securing and meeting a Kresge Foundation Challenge Grant can take more than two years.

- Maintain frequent communication with the foundation during the challenge grant phase.

*Source: Lee Mayhall, Vice President for College Relations, Development Office, Florida Southern College, Lakeland, FL. Phone (863) 680-4986. E-mail: lmayhall@flsouthern.edu*

*Make your grant proposal as strong as it can be, then let it sit for a few weeks to reveal any areas needing fine-tuning.*

## 10. Million-dollar Challenge Helps Build Endowment Fund

To help build a newly established endowment fund, a board member and chairman emeritus for the Character Education Partnership (CEP) of Washington, D.C., issued a challenge: "Raise $3 million, and I will gift $1 million."

The challenge came after extensive homework by persons doing the asking, says Lee MacVaugh, director of development and fundraising.

"This particular board member has been our chairman for 13 years and is very committed to our nonprofit. Because he has been so generous to our cause in the past, I wanted to make sure we weren't over-asking and burdening him with requests," says MacVaugh. "We came to the conclusion the ask should be for our newly created endowment fund.

"It only took him a few moments to ponder the idea before he issued the challenge," MacVaugh adds.

In a little over two months, the board member's challenge has led to four gifts totaling more than $150,000 and seven pledges from other board members.

"Meeting this challenge is very important for our organization," says MacVaugh. "I read once that donors like to give to organizations that are financially sound. If we can show $4 million in the bank, it will show prospective donors that CEP is financially secure and will be around for years to come."

He says the CEP has begun promoting the challenge through its website, mailings, donor meetings and annual report and will do so in future publications.

*Source: Lee MacVaugh, Director of Development and Fundraising, Character Education Partnership, Washington, D.C. Phone (202) 296-7743, ext. 14. E-mail: lmacvaugh@character.org*

*Ensuring that major donors are not overburdened helps ensure continued support for years to come.*

## 11. Approach $1,000-plus Prospects With Challenge Options

As you begin a new fiscal year and you're approaching $1,000-plus contributors for support, why not add some leverage to your ask by inviting them to establish a challenge gift at a higher level?

Since there are any number of types of challenges you could put forth, approach several of your past donors and $1,000-plus hopefuls with a menu of challenge concepts from which they can choose. After all, the more you engage a prospect in discussing and identifying a challenge gift opportunity that is appealing to him/her, the more likely he/she is to step up to the plate and establish a challenge gift. Think about it: Wouldn't you have a wonderful "problem" if three different people or businesses agreed to establish three different types of challenge gifts for your annual fund?

Perhaps one challenge would be to match any first-time gifts of $25 or more. Another might be to match any current and former board members who increase their giving by $500 or more. And a third donor could create a challenge gift that will match any current donors who increase this year's gift by 10 percent or more.

You have nothing to lose and everything to gain by exploring challenge gift ideas with your more generous donors and capable prospects. Any challenge gifts serve to leverage others' giving and can motivate the challenger as well.

### Challenge Gift Concepts to Consider

Here's a small sampling of the types of challenge gift concepts you could share with potential challengers. Match —

✓ All new and increased annual gifts.
✓ All board members (current and/or past) who increase their gifts.
✓ Past contributors who gave under $100 but choose to give at that level or higher this year.
✓ All businesses that make a first-time contribution.
✓ Anyone who increases their level of annual support to $1,000 and any first-time $1,000 contributors.
✓ Any lybunt or sybunt who gets back on board as a current contributor.
✓ Anyone who moves from one giving club level to the next.

## 12. Challenge Ideas

Does your organization make presentations to area civic clubs and organizations throughout the year? If so, why not get a challenge gift established that will match contributions from each audience member to whom you speak?

Who might put up the money to establish such a challenge? You might find a local civic club that would find such a challenge to be appealing.

## 13. Challenge by University President Boosts Faculty, Staff Gifts

In August 2007, Butler University President Bobby Fong challenged his faculty and staff to give $1 million to the Indianapolis, IN, university's ButlerRising "human capital" campaign before Dec. 31, 2007. As incentive, Fong offered to personally match, dollar for dollar, all faculty and staff gifts and pledges.

Faculty and staff rose to the challenge, raising an additional $479,172 in cash and pledges. This, added to the $630,000 they had already given since the start of the campaign in 2003, brought faculty and staff donations to a total of $1,130,825 — $434,000 of which was matched by Fong's challenge funds.

"Any time you have an opportunity to match gifts, you are successful," says Margy Nebesio, executive director of campaign programs. "A challenge match causes people to give a stretch gift because they only have to pay half of what it would cost for them to accomplish their giving goals."

The ButlerRising campaign, with a total goal of $125 million, is continuing to raise funds for endowed need-based scholarships, athletic facility improvements, an endowment of the Center for Faith and Vocation, and a 400-seat performance hall. Any faculty or staff donations given to these priorities were matched by the Fong challenge.

Fong is by no means the only member of the Butler staff to take the lead in bringing in support for the campaign. Chair of faculty giving, Roger Boop, a professor of education, rallied 21 donors with ties to the College of Education to give a total of $32,171 toward a needs-based, endowed scholarship for College of Education students by contributing the lead gift and asking his colleagues to participate. Many donors "stretched" and gave beyond their previous levels of support to earn Fong's matching funds, which brought the total raised to $59,595.

In addition, head women's soccer coach Tari St. John and her players challenged faculty and staff to support the campaign's athletic facility improvements by offering to match every $500 raised with $100 of St. John's own money. In a two-week period, they raised $2,600, for a total of $3,100 with St. John's match.

Faculty and staff donors were given baseball caps as thank-you gifts, and those who contributed a gift from August through December, were entered into a drawing to win prizes, such as reserved campus parking and tickets to performances.

In February, a faculty and staff celebration in Butler's historic Hinkle Fieldhouse honored all involved in the successful effort. The celebration included a buffet lunch, music and remarks from Fong, Boop and the vice president for advancement. The women's basketball coach who was campaign staff chair was on the road with the team, so Butler officials created a life-size cutout of her to stand on stage.

*Source: Margy Nebesio, Executive Director, Campaign Programs, Indianapolis, IN. Phone (317) 940-9712. E-mail: mnebesio@butler.edu. Website: www.butler.edu*

*Targeted challenges can be an effective way to reach specific constituencies such as staff, alumni or volunteers.*

# 14. Challenge Gift Concepts

As you consider different types of challenge gifts and whom you might approach to make them, give thought to an organization (a club or business) with many members or employees who, if your challenge is accepted, will get behind it and help you meet the goal.

One women's organization established a $250,000 challenge that would benefit a local nonprofit. Because all the club's members voted on whether to establish it, they all got behind it to see that the local nonprofit raised sufficient matching funds to qualify for the match.

Engaging the challenger's employees or members early on helps ensure they will get behind the effort and support it.

# 15. Know What's Important to a Foundation

For many corporations and foundations, selecting grantees is based somewhat on the process of elimination. With so many deserving requests, it becomes necessary to eliminate some, even though they may be well-written and worthy of funding.

Knowing what a foundation looks for can help you understand your organization's strengths and weaknesses and where you may need to make internal improvements.

Here are some common areas of interest that foundations consider as they prioritize possible grant recipients:

✓ **Track record of growth, achievement.** What has your nonprofit accomplished in fulfilling its mission? How has it distinguished itself from similar organizations?

✓ **Financial strength.** What does your most recent audit reveal? Have you achieved balanced budgets in recent years? Has gift support increased?

✓ **Diversity of funding base.** What are your sources of annual revenue? Who are your primary sources of gift support? Has your donor base broadened over time?

✓ **Active board.** Who makes up your board? Are they engaged and committed as both donors and volunteers?

✓ **Cash reserves.** Are you financially prepared for emergencies? Do you have an equipment and/or operations reserve?

✓ **Staff competency.** What is the quality of your top management? How long have they been with your nonprofit?

✓ **Program delivery.** Do you, in fact, provide the services you purport to provide?

✓ **Shared vision between staff and board.** Does the board support management's long-range plans?

✓ **Cost per unit of service.** What does it cost to provide a particular program? How many will benefit in relation to its cost?

✓ **Duplication of efforts.** Is another agency providing service(s) you hope to provide?

✓ **Comparison to a social cost.** How badly needed is the program in relation to other social services?

✓ **Degree of risk.** Can the project realize its aims if the funding is provided? Will the nonprofit survive the next decade?

*With granters looking for reasons to discard requests, perfection is crucial. Make sure every comma, period and dollar sign is in place!*

## 16. Board Chairman's Strong Belief Challenges Others to Give

In the midst of a comprehensive campaign for Lycoming College (Williamsport, PA), Chairman of the Board Arthur Haberberger and his wife Joanne proposed a new program to target donors who are considering their first outright major gift.

At Lycoming College the threshold for an endowed scholarship is $25,000. The Chairman's Challenge is an opportunity for prospective donors to establish a scholarship at the $20,000 level.

"The challenge is a generous commitment by the Haberbergers to help donors interested in starting a new scholarship reach the $25,000 minimum commitment," says Jennifer Wilson, director of development. "For every gift of $20,000, they will invest $5,000 toward a new endowed scholarship."

The couple has committed to seeing 50 new scholarships created, which, if realized, would mean $1.25 million in endowed scholarships for Lycoming. Since announcing the program in spring 2007, Wilson says they have averaged one new scholarship a month as a direct result of the challenge.

The development office works with the donor to develop the criteria (e.g., preference to students in certain academic fields or by geographic area). The name of the scholarship is also the donor's choice and can be named after a family member, in memory of a loved one, or themselves.

With the college in its active campaign solicitation, development office staff worked to identify potential scholarship donors through prospect meetings and talks with staff to identify prospects based on past giving and conversations with donors. "This challenge provided us a great opportunity to work with donors on taking the next step to a major gift," says Wilson.

They also marketed the program in the college magazine, campaign newsletter and in a brochure (shown below) developed specifically for the Chairman's Challenge as a leave-behind piece after solicitations.

Donors have the option to make their gift outright or fulfill their pledge commitment within three to five years.

*Source: Jennifer Wilson, Director of Development, Lycoming College, Williamsport, PA. Phone (570) 321-4395. E-mail: wilson@lycoming.edu*

Content not available in this edition

Content not available in this edition

## 17. Try a Group-challenge Gift

Challenge gifts are used all of the time to motivate others to give. Challenges include one-to-one matches, two-to-one matches, those that match all new and increased gifts and more.

For the most part, challenges generally come from one source — an individual, a foundation or a business.

Have you ever considered approaching a group of individuals to establish a challenge gift? Consider your board or, better yet, a group of up-and-coming philanthropists who have or one day will have the ability to make a major gift.

In addition to motivating others to increase their giving, a challenge of this sort will have another important benefit: It will provide a meaningful way to involve this group of challengers in your advancement efforts. By engaging them in this way, their ownership of your organization and its work will likely increase as well.

*Because of their relative rarity, group challenges can also be a good source of media coverage and attention.*

## 18. Individual School Endowment Initiative: 48 Schools, 48 Endowment Funds

The Foundation for Madison's Public Schools (Madison, WI) offered many giving options but lacked a vehicle for donors to support a particular school, says Martha Vukelich-Austin, foundation president.

All that changed in 2003 when one of the foundation's board members offered $5,000 challenge grants to establish endowment funds for each of the district's 48 schools. In the years since, the initiative has raised $1.66 million and built individual endowments ranging from $14,000 to $102,000.

Following the foundation's core mission, the Individual School Endowment Initiative primarily supports supplemental programming. "Revenue from the endowments provides funding for creative endeavors outside the district's core budget," says Vukelich-Austin.

Though the endowments are held and managed by an outside community foundation, Vukelich-Austin explains that annual disbursements (around five percent of each fund) are channeled to granting committees at each school. Working closely with a foundation liaison, these committees, consisting of the principal, staff and parents, review grant proposals and make recommendations to the foundation's board of directors.

Past funded proposals include purchasing software for a woodlands restoration project, acquiring materials for a map making/reading course and bringing artists in residence to various schools.

One of the initiative's biggest challenges is raising funds for all the schools, not just some, says Vukelich-Austin. But she adds that motivation is as important as financial resources, noting that the high school with the largest endowment also has the highest percentage of free and reduced lunches.

In 2010-2011 the endowments will provide $58,000 to the district, a more than four-fold increase over the first year's total of $14,000. Vukelich-Austin attributes such growth to strong parent support and an effective employee giving program. She adds that funding all endowments to $50,000 and linking each school with a community business partner are among the program's current goals.

*Community foundations can be a good choice for managing endowment funds, especially for smaller organizations.*

*Source: Martha Vukelich-Austin, President, Foundation for Madison's Public Schools, Madison, WI. Phone (608) 232-7820. E-mail: mvaustin@fmps.org. Website: www.fmps.org*

### 19. Keep the Challenger Up-to-date On Matching Gift Progress

Whenever you're fortunate enough to have a donor offer sufficient funds to establish a challenge gift, it's important to keep the donor informed throughout the challenge period. In addition to just being a good stewardship practice, doing so increases the odds of the challenger adding to his/her pledge or repeating it sometime.

Whether your periodic updates include correspondence, phone calls, personal visits or a combination of each, provide an ongoing printed report — such as the example below — that the challenger can use to get a quick read on the status of matching gifts. The frequency of updates should be based on the duration of the challenge period. If, for instance, the challenge covers a three-year period, quarterly updates might be appropriate. You may also choose to let the challenger decide how often he/she would like to review updates, and issue them accordingly.

*Regular updates can spur challenge donors to continue reaching out to personal friends and acquaintances.*

---

### Challenge Gift Update
### PREPARED ESPECIALLY FOR ALFRED M. WILSON
January 4, 2011

Challenge Start Date ___January 1, 10___  End Date ___December 31, 12___

| Challenge Rules: | Dollar-for-dollar match up to $1 million throughout the three-year period. Any gift directed to this project will be counted as a matching gift. |
|---|---|
| Use of Challenger's Gift: | To established The Wilson Leadership Symposium, an annual event that brings together some of America's top entrepreneurs who will publicly address key issues that impact the free enterprise system. |
| Use of Matching Gifts: | All matching gifts will be directed to The Wilson Leadership Symposium Endowed Fund. |

|  | Year 1 Amount/No. Donors | Year 2 Amount/No. Donors | Year 3 Amount/No. Donors |
|---|---|---|---|
| Apr | $  14,000 / 16 |  |  |
| Jul | $  48,000 / 37 |  |  |
| Oct | $  66,500 / 44 |  |  |
| Dec | $  89,000 / 43 |  |  |
| Total | $ 217,500 / 140 |  |  |

---

## 20. Big Gifts Require Monumental Dreams

As the well-known "Field of Dreams" movie line goes: "Build it and they will come." It's like that with giving as well: "Dream it and they will make it a reality."

But to attract unprecedented levels of giving, donors need to visualize and buy into big dreams of what could be. If those dreams don't exist and aren't shared, how can you ever expect to attract significant gifts?

As you formulate strategic plans for your nonprofit, help participants avoid small thinking. Share examples of other similar organizations that have made huge accomplishments as the result of principal philanthropic investments.

Remember, it's much easier to scale back a dream that can't get the necessary funding than it is to expand a small dream that can be easily funded.

## 21. Challenge Gift Encourages Alumni Giving

To help build a culture of annual giving at Worcester Polytechnic Institute (WPI), Worcester, MA, trustee and alumnus Mike Dolan is challenging alumni to support the institute by offering to match their $100-plus annual fund gifts, 50 cents on the dollar.

"I have a sense of obligation to pay back to the next generation what was so generously given to me," says Dolan, a chemical engineering major from WPI's class of 1975. "When I was a WPI student, there were people 20 or 30 years ahead of me who made contributions to build the buildings and hire the faculty that make WPI such a great place to learn."

The Dolan Challenge, which runs July 1, 2009, to June 30, 2010, is open to the 8,300 alumni from the classes of 1990-2009 who give $100 or more. As of April 23, 2010, 256 eligible alumni had made donations totaling $47,422, resulting in $23,711 in matching funds. The average gift was $185.

"This represents an eight percent increase in the average gift when fiscal year 2010 is compared to fiscal year 2009. Moreover, our retention rate has increased six percent between fiscal year 2008 and fiscal year 2010 (45 percent to 51 percent)," says Judith Jaeger, director of development communications.

In fall 2009, all 8,300 eligible alumni received a mailing about the challenge, says Jaeger. Of those alumni, 4,615 also received a call from WPI's student calling center and/or a personal visit from an annual fund staff member, she says. "These are people who meet a variety of criteria — generally they didn't respond to the mailings, we have their permission to call them, they may have given in the past but not the previous year, etc."

WPI development staff also sent several e-mails from their annual fund board chair at the end of the calendar year to promote end-of-year giving (for tax purposes) and the Dolan Challenge to those eligible for the match.

Inserts promoting the challenge were included in all mailings to challenge-eligible alumni, says Jaeger, who notes that those who participate receive a special acknowledgement letter from Dolan.

*Source: Judith Jaeger, Director of Development Communications, Office of Development and Alumni Relations, Worcester Polytechnic Institute, Worcester, MA. Phone (508) 831-5962. E-mail: jjaeger@wpi.edu*

*Donors with limited resources can stretch their challenge gift by matching at 75 or 50 cents on the dollar.*

## 22. Use a Challenge to Launch Your Major Capital Campaign

When you receive a life-changing gift, do all you can to maximize its impact.

When the United Way of Central Carolinas (Charlotte, NC) received an unsolicited $1 million matching challenge grant from the Leon Levine Foundation in support of its Community Care Fund Campaign just before the campaign kick-off, officials used the challenge grant to garner new support for the campaign by matching every dollar raised above the 2008 Community Care Fund amount.

"The grant added excitement, momentum and focus for our fundraising efforts this year," says Dani Stone, the United Way chapter's vice president of marketing. "Receiving this generous grant from the highly respected Leon Levine Foundation certainly helped us kick off our campaign in a very positive way. The grant provides a doubling effect for donors and provides an opportunity to set a new kind of goal — one that is focused on the Community Care Fund (undesignated dollars) from the outset, and not simply on the number of total dollars raised."

Focusing on the Community Care Fund, she says, helps provide a platform for continuity of the organization's core mission and helps build awareness and media coverage for the importance of supporting their local member agencies. One hundred percent of the dollars raised over last year's goal will go directly to the member agencies they serve.

Another reason for making the challenge grant part of the campaign kick-off, Stone says, was to begin soliciting companies that choose to participate in advance of pacesetter companies or at the very start of the United Way's official campaign season.

"We did not want to delay the announcement of the grant and miss opportunities with those donors and those workplace campaigns," she says. "The earlier we were able to share the announcement, the earlier we were able to focus on the Community Care Fund and ask donors to consider supporting it."

*Source: Dani Stone, Vice President of Marketing, United Way of Central Carolinas, Charlotte, NC. Phone (704) 371-6206. E-mail: dstone@uwcentralcarolinas.org*

*Challenge gifts can be a good way to direct resources to specific needs or programs.*

## 23. Challenge Gift Errors to Avoid

Challenge gifts can provide powerful benefits if used judiciously. But some organizations manage to challenge gifts haphazardly, and that's a mistake.

Avoid these challenge gift blunders:

- **Having challenge gifts too often.** Donors will become immune to challenges if you have them too often.

- **Concurrent challenges.** Challenges going on at the same time will impede, even confuse, people's motivation to give.

- **Challenges that don't appear genuine.** Many challenge gifts are set up so the donor agrees to make his/her gift even if the match fails to be met. That's wrong.

- **Challenges that are too complex.** Some challenges are set up with so many matching restrictions — what counts, what doesn't, or to whom the challenge applies — that people ignore them. Try to keep it simple.

- **Turning to too many donors for one challenge** — If you can't establish a generous challenge gift by going to one or a few sources, it may come across as meaningless to those being asked to match the challenge: "Why should we match a challenge gift that took 30 people to establish?"

*Remember, challenges are a motivation for staff as well. Avoiding errors keeps development officers at the top of their game.*

## 24. Identify Your Prospects' Response Motivators

What causes people to contribute to various causes? What motivates their gifts?

Response motivators are complex. The pathway leading from the "guttural" mechanism to an individual's choice of response is different for every person, depending on that individual's own life experiences. Yet, humans respond to a set of common psychological factors.

Knowledge of these response motivators can aid fundraising efforts and be used to positively reinforce donors in their decision to contribute.

Some examples of response motivators include, but are not limited to:

- **The ego factor** — All people seek attention and have the need to be recognized. Never underestimate the stroking power of named gifts, awards, special attention from your CEO and more.

- **The altruistic spirit** — Some individuals contribute purely for altruistic reasons, among the most noble of all. Donors among this group sometimes prefer to remain anonymous.

- **The desire for immortality** — Leaving a legacy becomes more important as we age. We look for ways to validate our existence and be remembered.

- **The need for safety** — Safety and security are essential for mental health. People need to feel they and those they care about are safe and secure. The missions of many nonprofits address these issues.

- **The need to belong** — Humans are social animals. Our identities are, in part, a result of the groups to which we belong with everyone aiming for connections of varying sorts.

*Response motivators are best used in formulating giving options. Avoid undue speculation about donors' personal motivations unless they share them.*

## 25. Challenge Gift Encourages Staff, Community Support

With aspirations of increasing physician, staff and public support for a new Princeton HealthCare System medical center (Princeton, NJ), a husband-and-wife donor team suggested a $25-million matching gift program.

"The donors, David and Patricia Atkinson, knew philanthropic support would be the difference in making this happen and suggested this matching gift program," says Joe Stampe, vice president of development.

The program has two components: the physician/staff challenge and the community challenge. The physician/staff challenge encourages hospital physicians and staff to support the construction project, by designating $5 million of the Atkinsons' pledge to be used as a one-to-one match.

"The Atkinsons' intent is to match any gift of $100 or more from a staff member or a staff physician one-to-one; meaning if a donor gives a gift of $1,000, the Atkinsons will match it with $1,000," explains Stampe.

The remainder of the pledge, $20 million, will be used as a one-to-two match. For example, if a donor gives $1 million, the Atkinsons will give $500,000.

Stampe says hopes are for the community challenge to raise $40 million. Both challenges run throughout the capital campaign's public phase.

*Source: Joseph Stampe, Vice President of Development, Princeton HealthCare System Foundation, Princeton, NJ. Phone (609) 497-4190. E-mail: jstampe@princetonhcs.org*

## 26. Avoid Burning Bridges When Answer Is No

Even when a major gift prospect denies your request for support or declines an opportunity for you to tell your story, do what is necessary to keep the door open.

You never know when a prospect might have a change of heart or shift in circumstances that would allow for reconsideration of your earlier request. "No" might really just mean "not now."

## 27. Campaign Makes All the Right Moves for Success

Supporters and friends of Gettysburg College had good reason to make a donation during March and April 2010 — the Cly-Del Challenge. The challenge matched, dollar-for-dollar, the first $150,000 in gifts made to the Gettysburg Fund, the Parents' Fund or the Orange & Blue Club during that time. It also offered an additional $50,000 incentive to attract 500 new alumni donors who had not made gifts this year or last. And it worked — the challenge was met with 2,400 donors making gifts of more than $630,000. Of those donors, 620 were making a gift for the first time in two years.

So what made it work? Susan Pyron, Assistant Vice President, Annual Giving, Alumni and Parent Relations, Gettysburg College (Gettysburg, PA) says challenges have always resonated with their donors and volunteers, but they did do a few things differently that really seemed to help.

First off, they really matched the needs of the challenge to the right donor. Pyron says donation amounts were holding steady, but participation was down, which was a concern. As a result, the college approached a high-profile alumnus and trustee, who chairs the enrollment and educational services committee and concerns himself with alumni involvement. His interest in keeping alumni involved matched well with the focus of the challenge, and he stepped up to make the gift.

By keeping the challenge period limited to two months, rather than trying to keep momentum up over a whole year, Pyron says it created a sense of urgency which also seemed to help.

Finally, Pyron says that thorough planning was also key. "We had a comprehensive marketing plan in place that was heavily coordinated with other departments. We also had the buy in and understanding of our entire division and the senior staff."

Selecting the right volunteers and expanding the use of social media were also important in the campaign's success.

*Source: Susan Pyron, Assistant Vice President, Annual Giving, Alumni and Parent Relations, Gettysburg College, Gettysburg, PA. Phone (717) 337-6542. E-mail: spyron@gettysburg.edu.*

---

### Six Techniques to Ensure Challenge Success

Susan Pyron, Assistant Vice President, Annual Giving, Alumni and Parent Relations, Gettysburg College (Gettysburg, PA) says several strategies, employed during different periods of their Cly-Del Challenge ensured the challenge's success. The following techniques were identified as the most important by Pyron:

- A committed volunteer base that is well trained and willing to reach out in the way deemed most effective by challenge staff.

- The inclusion of social media into the marketing mix.

- A high-profile, committed challenge donor who is well-matched to the needs of the challenge.

- A very condensed time to reach very specific goals.

- The buy in and understanding of key staff and departments achieved by involving them in the planning and utilizing them for challenge components.

- Heavy coordination of involved departments.

## 28. Challenge Gift Ideas

- To build membership in one of your gift clubs, secure a challenge gift to match all new contributions to that giving club.

## 29. Negotiating a Challenge Grant

A donor approaches you about making a large challenge grant, but you've never done one. You wonder: Will the challenge grant be worth the work involved?

Susan D. Smith, consultant, Susan D. Smith Consultant in Philanthropy (Barneveld, NY), says challenge grants are a great opportunity for attracting new and/or increased gifts, and, with good planning, can also provide the opportunity to leverage other gifts.

When presented with a proposed challenge gift or seeking to solicit one, Smith suggests that organizations begin by talking with the donor about what it is he or she expects the challenge to accomplish for the organization.

She says that including the donor in discussions about what the donor would like to see happen and the degree to which that is realistic and may be accomplished is important. "Is the donor envisioning that the challenge will spur gifts to the organization from people who have never given before? Does the donor wish to challenge a specific constituency (e.g., doctors in the region, alumni from 1962, current/past board members and other organization volunteers)? Does the donor hope the challenge will encourage increased gifts from those who regularly give?"

Other points to negotiate with the donor, Smith says:

✓ **Time to fulfill challenge.** Shorter-term challenges create a sense of urgency; if an organization has capacity and ability to bring in lots of gifts quickly, that might be a good way to go, she says: "I worked with a foundation that received a $500,000 challenge and was given 90 days to match it dollar-for-dollar. They did it, though it was a bit of a stretch. Challenges are good for those kinds of realistic stretches. Too long a time period to fulfill the challenge may not be best — the urgency is lost and potential donors forget about it.... A challenge that lasts more than six to 12 months may not be as effective as one that lasts three to four months."

✓ **The match ratio.** Challenges can be 1:1 (challenge matches donations dollar for dollar), 2:1 (challenge donor doubles each gift made by donor), 3:1, or even 4:1, she says. Or they can set a specific dollar goal. For example, if the organization can raise a specified percentage more than it typically does annually, or a specific dollar amount greater than what is usually raised, the donor will make his/her gift.

Be specific about what you are asking potential donors to do, says Smith: "Challenges are best when potential givers understand that the fate of the challenge gift depends on their acting. A challenge that says 'You'll get this no matter what, just do your best' isn't really the same kind of challenge as one that says 'In order to get my six-figure gift in full, you have to meet all the time conditions and dollar goals we agreed to and if you do not, the challenge goes away.' The urgency is what drives it."

*Source: Susan D. Smith, Consultant, Susan D. Smith Consultant in Philanthropy, Barneveld, NY. Phone (315) 896-8524. E-mail: sdsmith@ntcnet.com*

> *Match the challenge duration to its goal - the larger the amount the longer the time period that it will retain a sense of urgency.*

## 30. Challenge Gift Advice

- It's important to recognize that a challenge gift can motivate the challenger as much, sometimes more, as those expected to match the gift.

*Challenge gifts give phonathon callers a ready-made topic of discussion.*

## 31. Challenge Gift Helps Leverage Phonathon Pledges

Looking for ways to improve your phonathon's results? Secure a challenge gift that callers can include in their pitch.

A challenge gift that will match all new and increased gifts not only helps to leverage giving, it energizes callers as well.

Here's an example of how a challenge gift might be incorporated into a caller's script:

Caller: "I have exciting news to share! One of our agency's board members has established a $50,000 challenge this year. The board member will match, dollar for dollar, any first-time gifts or any increases over last year of up to $500 per donor.

"According to our records, Bill, you gave $100 last fiscal year. That means our challenger will match any increase you make up to $600 this year. Could you give $600 this year, Bill?"

Even if the person being contacted doesn't give the full ask amount, chances are they will respond to the challenge by making a first-time gift or contributing more than the previous year.

## 32. Multiple Challenges Spur Campaign Giving

Officials at St. Olaf College (Northfield, MN) raised more than $33.1 million in cash and pledges for a new science and mathematics building in its Beyond Imagination campaign that ended Feb. 21, 2008, seven months earlier than they anticipated.

One key to the campaign's success? The use of multiple challenges to encourage gifts from various groups, says Ron Bagnall, senior director of development.

One of those challenges, made by the 3M Foundation, raised more than $784,000 by encouraging employees and retirees of 3M with St. Olaf connections to make gifts to the campaign. Under the 3:1 challenge, the foundation matched the first $150,000 and then went even further, matching 1:1 gifts that exceeded the $150,000 fundraising goal and providing an additional $50,000 for meeting the challenge.

*To avoid confusion, try to direct concurrent challenges toward non-overlapping constituent groups.*

"Co-chair John Benson, a retired executive with 3M, was invaluable in opening the door and assembling a small committee to get the word out and solicit support from key donor prospects at 3M," Bagnall says.

Another challenge, made by an anonymous donor in December 2007, consisted of a 1:1 match, up to $3 million, of any new or increased gifts. The donor gave them an additional $500,000 for meeting the challenge.

"This challenge sparked a fire, allowing us to finish the campaign earlier than anticipated," says Bagnall. "Several board members increased their gifts as a result of the challenge." New donors also stepped up to help fill in mid-level donations, he says, noting that many of the gifts were $100,000-plus, with a few $25,000 gifts.

*Source: Ron Bagnall, Senior Director of Advancement, St. Olaf College, Northfield, MN. Phone (507) 786-3859. E-mail: bagnall@stolaf.edu*

## 33. Give Thought to Timing, Duration

Two key factors that play into challenge gifts are the timing and duration of the challenge. It's necessary that timing and duration fit your circumstances along with those of the challenge donor and those who might respond to the challenge.

Address these issues as you weigh the timing and duration of your challenge program:

✓ Will it be over the course of a calendar or a fiscal year (assuming they are different)?

✓ Will the challenge last for one year, three years or some other period of time?

✓ How will the timing of the challenge announcement fit in with existing fundraising efforts?

✓ Will the timing of the challenge gift be helped or impeded by any factors (other campaigns, the economy)?

✓ Will the timing of the donor's challenge and the ability of people to respond be optimal?

✓ Will the start and end dates of the challenge be the same for both the challenge donor and those who respond to the challenge?

*Major donors are usually happy to work with development staff to ensure optimal timing and roll-out of their gift.*

## 34. Final-push Efforts to Meet Your Goal

The challenge is to raise $100,000 in new and increased gifts throughout the current fiscal year. You've raised nearly $80,000 to date as you enter the fourth and final quarter of your year.

Will you make it? Now's the time to pull out every stop in your all-out effort to meet, even surpass the challenge-gift goal.

What can you do with just 90 days remaining before the end of your fiscal year? Consider any of these seven strategies:

1. Identify 40 people capable of making a $1,000 gift, knowing that half of them will need to respond to your invitation.

2. Get someone to underwrite the cost of a full-page ad in your local paper that describes the challenge and the impact it will have if you reach yhe goal.

3. Go back to everyone who has responded with a gift and ask them to consider a second gift.

4. Invite everyone who has responded to the challenge to extend an invitation to others to participate.

5. Offer a special premium to anyone who makes a gift during your final quarter.

6. Enlist volunteers to host several receptions in their homes or places of business for the purpose of publicizing your challenge and inviting attendees' participation.

7. Conduct a direct mail appeal to 1,000 or more nondonors asking for a $50 gift. Four-hundred responses at that level will result in the needed $20,000.

*Front-load your solicitation as much as possible, but know that challenge campaigns often come down to a few last days of feverish activity.*

## 35. Work to Land First-time Gifts From Businesses

Want to get more gifts from members of the business community? Create gift opportunities designed to get them on board. To secure more first-time gifts from businesses:

1. Share a menu of wide-ranging sponsorship opportunities. Offer a variety of sponsorship price tags.

2. Launch a business partners program that includes any business contributing $250 or more per year. Offer members some exclusive benefits to attract their participation.

3. Form a committee of existing business contributors to assist in identifying and calling on their colleagues.

4. Convince an existing business donor to establish a challenge gift aimed at nondonor businesses. Any first-time gift will be matched by the challenger.

## 36. Create a Plan for Approaching Challengers

So where do you begin when seeking a challenge gift? Whom should you approach? Here's a step-by-step approach you can follow:

1. **Identify a top-five list of prospects.** Who among your current donors a) as the capacity to make a five- or six-figure gift, even if it's over a period of three to five years and b) would be motivated by the publicity surrounding a challenge gift? If you're considering a business, consider the positive publicity you could generate that would place that business in a positive light. If you are considering an individual, give thought to the role ego might play in motivating a gift.

2. **Prioritize and personalize your top five.** Force yourself to prioritize who you will approach first, second and so on. Then develop a one- or two-page proposal that's tailored to each prospect. Your proposal should point out:

   • The rationale behind a challenge gift.
   • How the challenge will work and over what period of time the challenge will be in place.
   • How the challenger's gift will be used.
   • How the matching gifts from other donors will be used.
   • How the challenge will be promoted to the public.
   • The benefits to the challenger and how the challenge donor will be recognized once the challenge has been met.

3. **Systematically approach each challenge prospect.** Begin with your top prospect and explain that "we are approaching you as our top choice for the challenge donor, and here's why...." At the conclusion of your presentation, explain that because time is of the essence, it will be helpful to reach a decision by a particular date. By incorporating a reasonable deadline into your presentation, you can then move on to prospect number two if your initial request is rejected.

   If you have selected the right top five prospects, you will likely receive your challenge pledge at some point in the solicitation process. And even in those instances in which your invitation was rejected, you will have very likely solidified your organization's relationship with each would-be donor, thus increasing the likelihood of a generous gift at some point in the future.

*Don't be shy in setting a timeline for potential challenge donors. That sense of urgency will be needed in the campaign itself.*

## 37. Five Ways to Generate $25,000 More in Gifts

Could you use an additional $25,000 in annual gifts this year? Consider these ideas:

1. Organize a yearlong effort to **increase the number of $1,000 gifts by 25 donors.** Ask existing donors to help host receptions and invite support.

2. **Hold a new special event.** Assemble a group of committed and capable volunteers willing to coordinate a new fundraising event on behalf of your non-profit.

3. **Secure a $10,000 challenge gift.** Use it to match all new and increased gifts throughout the fiscal year.

4. **Identify a special funding project** that will compel new and existing donors to rise to the occasion. Assemble a group of volunteers willing to make calls; hold a special phonathon for the project; send an appeal to a targeted group of individuals/businesses on your mailing list.

5. **Develop a "business partners" club** that attracts support from area businesses and includes benefits that would appeal to this group: monthly partners' breakfast with a speaker, invitations to events; special benefits geared to businesses' employees.

*Challenge gifts can range in size, but should be large enough to capture the interest of your supporters.*

## 38. Presidential Connection Key to Challenge Success

At Agnes Scott College (Decatur, GA), President Elizabeth Kiss and her husband said they would match three-to-one every gift up to $3,000 that members of the senior class donated over six weeks. She did so with good reason, says Joanne Davis, director of the college's annual fund, "President Kiss has a special bond with the Class of 2010, because they were freshman the year she became president of Agnes Scott."

The Kisses also pledged to add an additional $1,000, for a combined total of $10,000, if the campaign reached a 90 percent participation level.

The president announced the challenge at the senior gift kick-off party and officially ended it at the senior dinner, sponsored jointly by the Alumnae Relations and Development offices. An e-mail sent to all seniors announced the challenge. Table times were held in the dining hall and signs were posted, encouraging seniors to make gifts.

The committee even held a Love President Kiss Day when seniors, students, faculty and staff received a heart cutout to pin on their clothing to show they had participated.

The connection between the president and senior class helped them surpass the $3,000 goal. Though they ended eight gifts short of 90 percent participation, Kiss announced at the senior dinner that the class would still receive the additional $1,000 because of their efforts to secure a record 110 gifts from faculty, staff and other students totaling $1,341. That $1,341 was in addition to the $3,040 they raised from the senior class.

*Source: Joanne Davis, Director of the Annual Fund, Agnes Scott College, Decatur, GA. Phone (404) 471-5343. E-mail: jadavis@agnesscott.edu*

*Combine participation and dollar-figure goals to achieve multiple objectives.*

## 39. Establish Challenge Gifts

Challenge gifts can be powerful tools to move would-be donors to donor status. Consider these and other challenge gift possibilities to boost your bottom line:

☐ **Individuals** — In addition to generating matching gifts, going to an individual for a challenge may help leverage a major gift as a result of the publicity it will generate. There's incentive for both the challenger and those responding to the challenge.

☐ **Groups of individuals** — Sometimes raising the needed challenge from one source is difficult. If that's the case, consider a challenge from group of participating donors.

☐ **Board challenge** — Get one board member to challenge the other board members or have the entire board establish a group challenge for your entire constituency.

☐ **Businesses** — Not unlike the publicity derived from sponsorships, businesses often value the positive exposure resulting from a challenge gift. Be sure your challenge proposal spells out those benefits to a business.

## 40. Use a Challenge Gift To Encourage Credit Card Giving

In 2009, officials at Salve Regina University (Newport, RI) boosted the overall credit card giving rate by phone from 14 percent to 22 percent by attaining an alumni challenge specifically for gifts made by credit card.

"We asked the donor if she would use her gift to offer this challenge and inspire credit card giving," says Brian Kish, assistant to the vice president for advancement.

"This donor is always looking for the best way to utilize her gifts to inspire others," Kish says. "She knew that we needed to improve in this area and was more than happy to have her gift leveraged in this manner."

The challenge gift ratio was slightly under 1:1, he says.

Kish shares the script university officials used to solicit gifts for this match:

*"That's great (NAME). Thank you very much. We really appreciate your gift to Salve Regina! Will that be on your MasterCard or Visa? This illustrates the 'assumptive ask' strategy.*

*If the donor says they don't want to use their credit card, the caller says: "We have just gotten word that one of our generous alumni has offered a challenge in which she will match any gifts made to the University on a credit card. With this in mind, would you like to accept her challenge by putting your gift on a credit card tonight?"*

Kish attributes the success of the challenge to the following:

1. Donors like to know that their gift can make a difference. "When they learn that their giving can make an even larger impact if they put it on a credit card, they usually tend to be encouraged by this idea," he says.

2. It is another reason supporting the case for credit card giving. Often, we just need more reasons to inspire giving whether it is on credit card or not.

3. It provided them with a polite way to ask again for a credit card. "Essentially a second ask," he says.

*Source: Brian Kish, Assistant to the Vice President for Advancement, Salve Regina University, Newport, RI. Phone (401) 341-2151. E-mail: brian.kish@salve.edu*

*Consider using a challenge as a way to make a second or increased-level ask.*

## 41. Appointment-setting Tip

■ When calling a prospect to set up an appointment, don't just hope — expect that a meeting will result from your call. Positive thinking improves your odds of success and helps you handle yourself with confidence.

## 42. Hard Work, Creativity, Combine to Meet Challenge Grant Requirements

Hospice of Southern Illinois, Inc. (Belleville, IL) had raised $5.5 million two-and-a-half years into its $7 million capital campaign to build the first licensed hospice home in Southern Illinois. But when the economy took a downturn, campaign organizers needed to find ways to re-energize campaign supporters and reach their campaign goal.

So Development Manager Susan Reilmann contacted the Kresge Foundation (Troy, MI) to be considered for a Kresge Challenge Grant. The Kresge Foundation selected Hospice of Southern Illinois as the recipient of a $400,000 challenge grant to be awarded if the hospice could complete its $7 million campaign by Dec. 1, 2009.

Reilmann says the hospice's capital campaign consultant, Dee Vandeventer of ME&V Fundraising Advisors (Cedar Falls, IA), was instrumental in their efforts to meet the Kresge Challenge. "Dee became affectionately known as my 'barking dog' and, when necessary, nipped at my heels to move me forward, particularly in the discouragingly low periods of production," she says.

Together Reilmann and Vandeventer came up with several strategies for meeting the Kresge Challenge, including:

✓ Updating and creating more enticing naming opportunities, e.g., "Every time a patient's family opens the door to this armoire, your heart will open with joy knowing you have helped create a comfortable environment in a difficult time in their life."

✓ Ramping up their roster of scheduled speaking engagements at which they showed a mission-driven, needs-based video created by ME&V Consultants.

✓ Taking advantage of local bank presidents' contacts by inviting them to lunch and sharing insider campaign information that they could then share with constituents.

✓ Leveraging other challenge grants by asking the community to "Help make sure these challenge dollars aren't lost" or "You can make all the difference in helping us earn these challenge dollars." They used public challenge donors to create friendly rivalries with persons they knew had a relationship with the challenge donor.

✓ Asking board members to make thank-you calls to $1,000-plus donors. "Not only did this effort have a powerful impact on many of the donors, it ultimately sealed a few lifelong gifts via planned giving options," she says. "The most frequent comments from donors were 'Seriously — you're not calling to ask for additional money?' and 'Wow, I've never had a board member call — often a staff person which is great, but a board member? Thank you in return for your acknowledgement.'"

✓ Launching a church campaign. Hospice officials asked local churches to make the hospice the recipient of discretionary funds they set aside for special

*The motivation inherent in a challenge gift sometimes needs to be augmented with naming and recognition opportunities.*

*Continued on pg. 26*

*Continued from pg. 25*

community projects. They also solicited individual church members through meetings with church sub-groups, church bulletins, flyers, and by adding a donation envelope at a worship service where hospice officials were invited to speak. "After hearing about the support offered by their church, many individuals and families contacted us to make personal pledges and donations because they felt if their church endorsed our hospice home, it was worthy of their support," says Reilmann.

One week before the Kresge Challenge deadline, Reilmann used this final strategy to raise the remaining $35,000 needed to fulfill challenge stipulations: She made a personal call to a firm that her campaign team felt could have given more. "I issued them a personal challenge to help us raise the remaining $35,000 in the next week and in return they would receive a big media splash that said congratulations to their company for helping us make the final goal. With the backing of the principals in the firm, they ended up raising nearly $50,000 in that final week. Their strategy was to give each donor a day off during the holidays for each donation or pledge of $1,000 or more."

Reilmann shares a final piece of advice: "Don't be afraid to find and use that vulnerable spot in a company's public image by giving them a way to shine it. Always find a way to make individual donors feel good about your organization and how they can help."

*Source: Susan Reilmann, Development Manager, Hospice of Southern Illinois, Inc., Belleville, IL. Phone (618) 235-1703. E-mail: sreilmann@hospice.org*

*Religious organizations are an often-overlooked source of potential support, particularly in challenge campaigns.*

## 43. Client Challenge Creates Opportunity For Annual Campaign

How can you challenge your donors to add more funds to your annual campaign?

When a young client brought a homemade apple pie to radio personalities running the annual radiothon for the Make-A-Wish Foundation® of the Mid-South (Memphis, TN), she had no idea how much support she would end up generating for the campaign.

Off the cuff, the personalities posed a challenge: What if the young chef — a youngster who had her wish granted by the nonprofit — sold her homemade pies for $500 apiece? The child took that challenge and easily sold more than 20 pies.

The pie challenge has become a regular part of the campaign, with approximately 10 pies being sold, raising enough money to grant the wish of a child every year.

*Source: Liz Larkin, President/CEO, Make-A-Wish Foundation of the Mid-South, Memphis, TN. Phone (901) 680-9474. E-mail: llarkin@midsouth.wish.org*

*When given adequate support and direction, children and youth can elicit significant financial support.*

## 44. Challenge Gift Idea

To reach first-time donors and nurture annual giving, have someone establish a challenge gift that matches first-timers' initial and repeat gifts over three years.

## 45. Old Friends Lead the Way With Milestone Gift

You've probably heard the saying, "Make new friends, but keep the old...." And that's just what officials at the Stuhr Museum Foundation (Grand Island, NE) did with great success in their annual fund challenge.

Kristen Eckhardt, annual giving director, says they approached the law firm of Shamberg, Wolf, McDermott and Depué (Grand Island, NE) to provide the challenge gift for the 2010 campaign.

"Partner Ron Depué served on the museum's operating board and the foundation board for a total of 17 years, so we had a very strong connection," Eckhardt says. "Even before that, the law firm and museum have had a long history together, from the museum's founding days in the 1960s."

That connection led the firm to pledge $12,500, commemorating 125 years of practice by giving $100 for each year.

Museum staff named the challenge the New Friends, Old Friends Challenge, which tied into the campaign's theme of Stuhr Museum Needs Friends Like You!

New friends (new donors) who gave $100 or more had gifts matched, as did old friends (returning donors) who increased their last annual fund drive gift by $100 or more. The law firm would match both categories combined, up to $12,500.

The dual nature of the challenge was intentional, says Eckhardt. "Our challenge last year was to recruit new donors (which met with great success), and we wanted to build on that by engaging both returning donors and brand-new donors."

The strategy seems to have paid off, with 26 percent of donors meeting the challenge. Overall, the campaign raised $182,832 (102 percent of the $180,000 goal) from 460 donors.

*Source: Kristen Eckhardt, Annual Giving Director, Stuhr Museum Foundation, Grand Island, NE. Phone (308) 385-5131. E-mail: keckhardt@stuhrmuseum.org*

*If your challenge aims to bring in new donors, have plans in place to integrate and steward those new supporters.*

## 46. Share a List of Challenge-gift Opportunities

Why do so many nonprofits have challenge gifts in place? Simple answer: they work. Especially during these economic times, anything you can do to motivate giving is a plus, and challenge gifts help to leverage giving.

Knowing the power of a challenge gift, there's no reason why you can't attempt to have multiple challenge gifts — directed to different groups and for different reasons — going at the same time. The key is finding donors willing to establish the challenge.

To focus on getting multiple challenge gifts in place, why not create a simple brochure describing a number of different types of challenge gift opportunities? Share it with individuals, businesses and foundations capable of making significant challenges.

Use the sample list shown here as a starting point to create your own list of challenge gift opportunities, then begin meeting one on one with your top 50 prospects and invite them to select a challenge opportunity that best suits their interests.

### Challenge-gift Opportunities

Select from among these and other challenge-gift opportunities as a way to support [name of organization] in a major way and motivate others to support our efforts as well.

Keep in mind that the challenge opportunities shown here can be tailored to fit your wishes: payout period, use of your gift, challenge criteria and more.

**Who you might challenge**
- Anyone
- Board members
- Alumni or a particular group of alums
- Nondonors
- Businesses
- Churches
- Particular professions (attorneys, retailers)

**How your gift might be used**
- Annual fund support (general operations)
- Named endowment gift
- Special project (See examples)

**How matching gifts might be used**
- Annual fund support (general operations)
- Endowment
- Special project (See examples)

**Challenge gift criteria (what gets matched)**
- New, first-time gifts
- Increased gifts
- Gifts of a certain threshold ($1,000 and up)

## 47. Explore a Multipurpose Challenge

When drafting a multiyear challenge proposal, consider structuring the challenge to target different audiences for different purposes.

To illustrate, here's an example of a three-year challenge aimed at two groups of would-be donors:

**Total Challenge:** $60,000 ($20,000 per year for three years)

*Board Component* — $30,000
The challenger agrees to match all individual board member gifts that increase by more than $500 — up to $10,000 per year for three years.

*Nondonor Component* — $30,000
The challenger agrees to match all first-time gifts up to $10,000 per year for three years.

## 48. Challenge Aims to Increase Recent Grad Participation

In an effort to increase participation by recent graduates, officials with Hamline University (St. Paul, MN) launched a month-long challenge to nondonors who graduated between 1997 and 2007.

Molly Bass, assistant director, annual giving programs, says that during a brainstorming session with colleagues and the alumni annual fund board of directors, they reached a consensus of the importance of getting recent graduates on board financially. So they took action.

"With nearly one-third of graduates from the last decade making up our alumni base, we recognized that this group is an incredible resource with great potential," says Bass. "In many ways they are the future of the university. Getting this group involved in Hamline, through volunteer work or financial support, will influence how much we are able to grow."

Karla Williams, director of annual giving, presented the idea of the Gold Challenge to the alumni annual fund board. The board, in turn, agreed to match dollar for dollar any gift of $10 or more made by nondonors March 1-31.

To market the challenge, university staff created a series of five e-cards and two postcards. The university's call center also called this group for three weeks, while class agents from 1997 through 2007 sent personal e-mails and postcards to the target group.

"We knew we had to be creative and responsive with this group," says Bass. "Graduates for the last 10 years desire and expect more than traditional fundraising pieces. They like choices and want to be able to easily make their gifts online and this series of five e-cards — one every Tuesday during March — gave them the ability to direct their gift to an area that matters to them."

The challenge resulted in more than 60 new donors and more than $2,500 raised (before matching funds). Bass notes that it was interesting to find out that in terms of distance, the closest gift came from her office — a young alumna who works in alumni relations — and the gift from the greatest distance came from Brussels. Both gifts were made online.

*Source: Molly Bass, Assistant Director, Annual Giving Programs, Hamline University, St. Paul, MN. Phone (651) 523-2787. E-mail: mbass01@hamline.edu*

*Give your challenge every chance for success by developing attractive, donor-targeted promotional materials.*

## 49. Challenge Aims at Getting New, Increased Gifts

To continue to successfully raise funds in the current economic downturn requires creativity and innovation.

Early this year, members of the Stuhr Museum of the Prairie Pioneer and Foundation's development committee (Grand Island, NE) realized that because of the economy, soliciting gifts for the museum's annual fund could be especially challenging.

So instead of asking their loyal donors to increase their gifts in the tough economic times, they decided to target new or renewed donors.

The goal of the foundation's "A Time Like No Other..." campaign is to attract 550 new or increased donors in 2009, a 16 percent increase (75 donors) over the 2008 campaign, which attracted 475 donors. The dollar goal remains the same as 2008: $180,000.

Giving early momentum to the effort, an anonymous donor has also pledged a $15,000 challenge match for new donors. (New donors are defined as those who have never contributed to the museum's annual fund and renewed donors are defined as lapsed donors who have not contributed for at least one year.)

The campaign kicked off in March with a closing date of mid-July. Gifts normally continue to come in beyond mid-July, and are still credited to the campaign through Dec. 31 of the campaign year, says Pam L. Price, the foundation's executive director.

"We typically end up quite a bit over the public goal," she says. "For instance, in 2008, we announced on July 17 that we had reached (and surpassed at 107 percent) our fundraising goal of $180,000, raising $193,370 from 442 donors. By Dec. 31, we had raised $203,363 from 475 donors."

As of May 27, 2009, Price says, they had raised $139,714 in gifts and pledges from 379 donors. They had attracted a total of 97 new and renewed donors (40 new and 56 renewed). At this same time last year, she says, they had raised $159,877 from 379 donors.

"Since we have the exact number of donors — 379 — that we had at this time last year but have raised $20,000 less, this reinforces our decision to target new and renewed donors and use the 'A Time Like No Other...' theme for our 2009 campaign," Price says.

Twenty-two of this year's new and renewed donors have come on board as a direct result of the "progressive strolls" that take place in Stuhr Museum's recreated 1890s Living History Railroad Town, says Price. She notes that the events have also helped bring in 17 new memberships to the museum this year to date.

The strolls, which are designed to make people aware of the museum and its programs, include an ask, says Price. "While those making the ask explained the foundation would mail campaign materials within the next two to three days, we also had pledge cards and membership materials on hand."

If they had not made their financial goal by late June, plans were to mail what is referred to internally as "Last Gasp" appeal to everyone who has been solicited but has not yet given, the foundation executive director says: "While we have already made our 'challenge' goal, it looks like we will need to mail this last appeal in order to make our financial goal by mid-July."

To see where the campaign currently stands, visit the museum website at www.stuhrmuseum.org.

*Source: Pamela L. Price, Executive Director, Stuhr Museum Foundation, Grand Island, NE. Phone (308) 385-5131. E-mail: pprice@stuhrmuseum.org*

*Emergency plans (made well ahead of time) for the final weeks of your challenge can mean the difference between success and failure.*

# 50. Challenge Gift Approaches

- Think about your giving constituency. Do you have difficulty identifying one person or business you feel you can approach for a major challenge gift? Consider a group challenge in which a certain number of individuals agree to pledge a particular amount to comprise a significant challenge gift.

# 51. Consider Attaching a Challenge to a Major Gift

Do you have someone nearly ready to make a major gift? If the gift is a forgone conclusion, why not use all or a portion of it to establish a challenge for additional gifts?

Approach the donor and emphasize the enhanced value that could be realized with this major gift. Explain to the donor how earmarking the gift — or a portion of it — or an addition to it — as a challenge gift would encourage others to give.

Challenge gifts help motivate others to give, so any time a donor comes through with a major gift, explore possible challenge opportunities that may exist.

*Basing challenge levels on past performance keeps goals realistic and gives focus to the planning process.*

# 52. Challenge Can Generate Donations During Slumps

Gift challenges, growing in popularity among educational institutions, can be a successful way for all nonprofits to encourage giving.

Shaké Sulikyan, director, annual giving and alumnae relations, Pine Manor College (Chestnut Hill, MA), says a general participation challenge helped to more than double their number of monthly donors in May 2008. Here's how it worked:

As part of the college's fiscal year 2008 final-push strategy, the college implemented the May Challenge. The goal was to get 200 donors in the month of May. If the goal was met, a donor had promised to give an additional $20,000. There were no restrictions on who the donors could be.

Says Sulikyan, "An analysis showed that for each of the past five years, the only month we had more than 200 donors was December. Most months we have less than 100 donors, so this was a real stretch for us."

Sulikyan promoted the challenge through postcards sent out to all alumnae, parents and friends who had given to the college in one or more of the fiscal years 2005, 2006 and 2007, but had not yet given to the 2008 annual fund; an announcement in an alumnae e-newsletter; and an e-mail sent to faculty and staff. A website, updated daily, tracked the progress of the challenge. Phone program callers mentioned the challenge during each call, which also helped with credit card donations. Finally, they sent out an e-mail to all nondonors four days before the deadline of the challenge letting them know they needed 43 more donors to reach the goal.

In the end, the college exceeded the goal with 245 donors giving a total of $59,391.

*Source: Shaké Sulikyan, Director, Annual Giving and Alumnae Relations, Pine Manor College, Chestnut Hill, MA. Phone (617) 731-7099. E-mail: ssulikyan@hotmail.com*

## 53. Secure a Multiyear Challenge

Rather than a single year challenge gift, work at securing a multiyear challenge that can be used to match new and increased gifts over a three- to five-year period.

Multi-year challenge benefits include:

✓ Maximizing the challenge gift.
✓ Leveraging new and increased gifts over a multiyear period.
✓ Building a yearly habit of giving among new contributors.

## 54. Regularly Review Your Top 100 Individual Prospects

Your top 100 prospects represent a dynamic, ever-changing group of individuals.

To properly rank and steward this important group, review your list regularly — at least monthly — and prioritize who should remain, who should be added and who should be moved to a lower priority (or inactive) level.

Include in this review process criteria related to both capability and inclination to give.

Give staff and highly involved board members a list of your current top prospects, along with additional names not presently on that list. Instruct those persons to first review the list individually, assigning a rating of 1, 2 or 3 beside each prospect's name — 1 meaning keep on the list, 2 meaning discuss for possible change in status, and 3 meaning recommendation to add to the list.

Then meet as a group, and compare your thoughts and adjust your top-100-prospect list accordingly.

*Regularly assessing top prospects keeps your organization ready to meet unforseen financial challenges.*

## 55. Keeping Challenge Simple Offers Big Gain

The challenge was a simple one — if 10,000 donors made a gift of any amount to Skidmore College (Saratoga, NY) by May 31, 2010, Susan Kettering Williamson, trustee and co-chair of the Creative Thought, Bold Promise campaign would add $1 million to her own gift.

The idea was to increase the number of donors giving to Skidmore, and the effort worked, says Lori Eastman, director of development, who says, "One out of four of our donors today did not make gifts to Skidmore last year."

Development staff started marketing the challenge in September 2009 through communications efforts, volunteer programs and student calling. They increased Web and e-mail outreach to include both monthly challenge updates and additional online appeal reminders.

Helping boost those efforts were more than 125 new alumni volunteers who helped reach out to prospective donors, says Eastman. "That gave us the opportunity to contact an additional 1,000-plus classmates with peer-to-peer outreach. One of our graduates was so enthusiastic about the challenge he offered to help us with a marketing and communications effort."

In the end, the college received gifts from 11,215 donors and secured the $1 million challenge gift. Eastman says it is the simplicity that made the most difference. "It's very important to keep it simple. We were helped by the fact that there wasn't a complicated formula to having your gift matched."

*Challenge gifts can be multifaceted, multidonor, multi-year — but they don't have to be. Don't be afraid to keep things simple!*

*Source: Lori Eastman, Director of Development, Skidmore College, Saratoga Springs, NY. Phone (518) 580-5647. E-mail: leastman@skidmore.edu*

## 56. Challenge Gift Ideas

**Reverse challenge** — Under normal circumstances, you would secure a generous challenge gift from one donor and then attempt to find matching dollars from multiple contributors. But what if the reverse was true? Let's say you have 10 individuals each willing to put up $1,000 if you can find one $10,000 donor. Those 10 pledges could then be used as leverage to convince someone to make a $10,000 gift.

Whenever establishing a challenge gift, remember that motivation can work in both directions.

## 57. Challenge Makes History, Helps Keep Campaign Momentum Going

*When conducting a multi-part challenge, only discuss those aspects that pertain to any given donor.*

Riding the momentum of a recent capital campaign, a giving challenge made to parents of students attending Blair Academy (Blairstown, NJ) broke records for the private boarding school.

"We had just come off a campaign and wanted to keep the momentum going," says Sue Habermann, director of capital giving and past director of parent relations, of the challenge. "Many times schools start challenges later in the year if they aren't meeting goals, but we decided to start ours at the beginning of the school year to keep that campaign energy going and invigorate our volunteers."

An anonymous group of Blair parents issued a challenge for other parents by establishing a $200,000 challenge grant for the 2009-10 school year, she says. "In the past, we have had tremendous success from our parents who see the direct results of their children's education. This challenge gave parents not only another reason to support the students, but also the incentive to boost their annual fund participation to a new level."

Specifically, Habermann says, the challenge:

- Matched new gifts dollar-for-dollar up to $2,000.
- Generated an additional $500 for increased gifts of any size.
- Included a $10,000 gift added to any first-time gift of $10,000 or more.

What advice does Habermann have for challenge campaign success? "Simplify. It's important to make it easy to understand," she says. "When calling potential donors, only talk to them about how the challenge would apply to them."

School officials informed parents of the challenge through the school's fall appeal, parent newsletter, website and a special meeting on Parents' Weekend. Habermann says the most successful method for sharing the challenge information was by parents calling other parents.

Initiated in October 2009, the challenge ran through June 2010, which was six months longer than originally planned, Habermann says, noting: "The challenge was going so well, so the school approached a donor and asked if (he/she) would be willing to extend it."

She says results exceeded Blair officials' expectations, with the parent challenge raising $337,474 in matching funds. Sixty-one percent of current parents increased their gift from the prior year and 78 percent of new parents made a gift. Also, 20 parents each gave a first-time gift of $10,000.

The challenge also helped the school make history, pushing Blair Fund parent giving past the $1 million mark for the first time, to a record $1,110,408 with 81 percent participation.

*Source: Sue Habermann, Director of Capital Giving, Blair Academy, Blairstown, NJ. Phone (908) 362-6121, ext. 5653. E-mail: habers@blair.edu*

## 58. Closing Techniques

- The **comparative close** — Be ready to share anecdotes of donors who have made similar gifts for similar purposes. Sharing like but real examples of major gifts helps the prospect overcome reluctance to make a major gift investment.

## 59. Ask High and Negotiate Down

If you ask donors for a specific amount, but they say they can't afford that, don't be afraid to negotiate down, says Jean Block, president, Jean Block Consulting, Inc. (Albuquerque, NM): "Say to them, 'I understand. If $10,000 is too much, would you be willing to look at other opportunities?'"

*Source: Jean Block, President, Jean Block Consulting, Inc., Albuquerque, NM. Phone (505) 899-1520. E-mail: jean@jblockinc.com*

## 60 $30 Challenge Widens Appeal of Naming Campaign

Naming opportunities are often reserved for major donors, but they don't have to be. Spread access to this unique benefit (and boost your total revenue) by challenging supporters to pool their resources.

"About a year ago, one of our alums came to me and said that he couldn't afford to name a room for $3,000, but he could afford to purchase a $25 to $30 raffle ticket for a chance to furnish a room," says Carrie Williams, director of alumni relations at the Marion Military Institute (Marion, AL), whose Annual Fund Campaign, ROOM TO GROW!, is part of a comprehensive plan toward the renovation of all of the rooms in the barracks.

"Encouraged by his idea, we created the $30 in 30 Days Challenge, a short mini-campaign that gave lower-level donors the chance to name a room."

A gift of $30 or more ($60 gave the donor two chances, and so on) entered the donor into a drawing for the chance to name a room. The class year that gave the most was also recognized with a room. "We had former classmates encouraging fellow classmates to give," she says. The drawing was held at the Institute's Alumni Weekend at the end of April.

Most of the promotion for the challenge was done through word-of-mouth, e-mail blasts, the Institute's website, and using Facebook and Twitter. They also mailed a postcard, which was produced, printed and mailed in-house.

"Our message was that although $30 couldn't refurbish a room, their $30 combined with 100 others could," she says. The challenge raised $10,920 from 144 donors. "It got quite a buzz going, especially with our younger alumni," says Williams. "It was one of our most exciting campaigns."

The $30 in 30 Days Challenge was so successful, they held a second one called $100 in 100 Days Challenge, in which a drawing was held every 33 days and three donors were selected to name rooms. The $100 in 100 Days Challenge raised $9,175 from 44 donors.

"We will probably do it again," says Williams. "It was easy, cost-effective and didn't take up a lot of time."

*Source: Carrie Williams, Director of Alumni Relations, Marion Military Institute, Marion, AL. Phone (334) 683-2350. E-mail: cwilliams@marionmilitary.edu*

*Don't overlook the impact lower-lelvel donors can have by pooling their resources!*

## 61. Consider a Letter as a Way To Introduce Challenge Concept

Although nothing beats a face-to-face visit whenever you are selling something, there may be times with an introductory letter will help to set the stage for a visit that follows.

Consider the possibility of using a personal letter to introduce the notion of a challenge gift from a prospective donor.

---

*Harriman Academy*

Mr. Max Tiggler
30 White Pines Dr
Colorado Springs, CO 81521

Dear Max:

Although we want to discuss this matter with you in person, I thought it might be helpful to introduce the idea of a Challenge Gift to you by letter, as a way for you to think about the idea and how it might work, prior to our meeting.

Specifically, I would like to invite you to consider a Challenge Gift of $150,000 — $50,000 each year for three years — that we could use as a way to motivate others to support our Annual Fund effort.

Here's how such a Challenge Gift might work: Beginning next July, the beginning our fiscal year, we would publicly announce your Challenge Gift, pointing out that it will be used to match all new and increased gifts — up to $50,000 each year for the next three years — directed to our Annual Fund.

|  | Year 1 | Year 2 | Year 3 |
|---|---|---|---|
| Challenge Gift | $50,000 | $50,000 | $50,000 |
| Matching Gifts | $50,000 | $50,000 | $50,000 |

Your $150,000 gift would be used to establish a named endowment fund, and those gifts given in response to your Challenge would be used to support our general operations.

I truly believe a Challenge Gift such as this would help to inspire non-donors to consider a first-time gift and motivate existing donors to increase their level of support, resulting in an additional $50,000 per year in additional funding for our general operations.

Equally important, your gift will be used to establish a named endowment fund, the annual interest of which would be used to fund a program of our mutual choosing (e.g. endowed scholarship) for generations to come.

I come to you, Max, based on your belief in our academy and what we hope to accomplish. There are few who could establish a Challenge Gift such as this.

Please give thoughtful consideration to this invitation, and I will plan to contact you within the next two weeks to set a time and place where we can explore this further.

Sincerely,

Emily H. Harris
Vice President for Advancement

---

A letter can be advantageous in several ways:

1. It introduces the idea of a challenge gift in a more palatable way, giving the would-be donor time to consider the possibility of a challenge gift.

2. A letter can set the tone for your eventual visit and point out why you think this individual (or business) would make an ideal candidate as a challenge gift donor.

3. Your letter can serve to educate the donor about how this particular challenge gift might work: use of donor's gift, use of matching gifts, duration of challenge and so forth. It establishes a framework around which discussions can emerge.

Because there are so many variations of challenge gifts — matching ratio, what counts, what doesn't count, duration of challenge, use of gifts — a letter helps the would-be donor visualize how it all might come together.

A critical ending to your letter: Include a call to action stating you will contact the individual within a specified period of time to set an appointment and discuss the idea in more detail.

*Sample Introductory Letter*

## 62. Negotiating Tip

- If a prospect tells you he will pledge $150,000 over a three-year period, but you were hoping for more, ask whether extending the payout period for another two years would help maximize his/her ability to do more. At $50,000 per year, that's another $100,000.

## 63. Challenge Gift Idea

If your annual donor base is much smaller than you'd like, why not ask all current donors to establish a collective challenge that will match all first-time gifts?

One West Coast library's friends group put up a challenge to do just that, collectively pledging to match up to $10,000 in any new gifts that came in throughout the library's fiscal year.

## 64. Foundation Challenge Gifts Help Carry Momentum

Once you have at least 50 percent of your campaign goal in hand, and you have announced the public phase of your campaign, consider going after challenge grants from foundations (e.g., Kresge Foundation) to help carry you through to the end.

A challenge grant from a foundation has threefold benefits:

1. Putting your foundation proposal in the form of a challenge may be what it takes to secure the foundation grant.

2. Doing so can help motivate new pledges throughout your campaign's public phase.

3. In addition to new pledges, you may be able to make return visits to those who made lead gifts, inviting them to increase their pledges in response to the challenge grant.

*Collaborating with foundations can be a lengthy process. Consider submitting a proposal before your campaign has even begun.*

## 65. For Challenge Success, Keep It Simple, Advertise

*Q. What tips do you have for someone looking to implement challenge campaigns?*

"Make sure the terms of the challenge are simple — the simpler the better (e.g.; the donor will match all gifts received between Jan. 1 and Feb. 15 one-to-one, or the donor will match all new gifts on a one-to-one basis).

"Also, make sure you advertise it as much as possible. We sent out a postcard to announce our last challenge but didn't provide a response device, so the money came in rather slowly at first. A staff member designed a card explaining the terms of the challenge. After we began inserting that card in fund chair letters and in student calling program pledges, the money came in faster because both had business return envelopes enclosed."

*Source: Joanne Davis, Director of the Annual Fund, Agnes Scott College, Decatur, GA. Phone (404) 471-5343. E-mail: jadavis@agnesscott.edu*

*As in all fundraising efforts, make it as easy as possible for supporters to respond to a challenge campaign.*

## 66. Video Thank-you Delivers Message For $5M Challenge Success

To thank all donors — especially those who helped reach an unprecedented $5 million alumni challenge gift from an anonymous donor — the annual fund team at Trinity College (Hartford, CT) turned to the college's communications team.

The result is a video showing those persons most impacted by donors' generosity — students with a wide range of academic and social interests — shown in locations throughout campus as they say, "Thank you!"

Director of Annual Giving Jocelyn Kane says the video included a personal thank you from the college president and a whimsical story line featuring the college's mascot, the Trinity Bantam, presenting the president with a briefcase holding the $5 million.

The communications team created the video in-house using available equipment. The only external cost was $25 in music copyrights through a third-party website.

All alumni donors received an e-mail with a link to the video on YouTube (http://www.youtube.com/watch?v=331ndHIcAU0). If no e-mail address was available, donors were sent postcards with the video's website address. The link is also posted on the college website, www.trincoll.edu.

*Source: Jocelyn Kane, Director of Annual Giving, Trinity College, Hartford, CT. Phone (860) 297-2367. E-mail: jocelyn.kane@trincoll.edu*

> *A video tribute can be a powerful way to thank both the source of a challenge and the donors who responded to it.*

## 67. Combat Major Donor Fatigue With Challenge Gifts

Major donors can grow tired of being the only one giving large gifts on a regular basis, says Elizabeth Outland Branner, director of law school advancement at Washington and Lee University School of Law (Lexington, VA). "They want to support the institution they care about, but they also want to know who else is stepping forward."

Challenge gifts can be a powerful way to address such fatigue.

Such was the case in recent conversations that resulted in a $2 million gift supporting W&L Law's new third-year program. "A long-time donor was open to a major gift supporting this program, but he wanted to know what we were doing to get other people involved," says Branner.

In response, Branner suggested structuring part of the donation as a challenge gift, thereby providing both an example for others to emulate and a tool for advancement officials to enhance solicitation efforts. The donor consulted with his wife and eventually chose to provide $1.5 million in direct support, with an additional $500,000 to match supporting gifts, 50 cents on the dollar.

The arrangement — and the challenge element in particular — proved to be a source of great satisfaction for the donor. "He has been very enthusiastic about the number of smaller donors that are stepping forward," says Branner. "The challenge is structured so that we could meet it with one big donation, but he is much more interested in generating many small gifts from a greater number of alumni, and that's just fine with us."

*Source: Elizabeth Outland Branner, Director of Law School Advancement, Washington and Lee University School of Law, Lexington, VA. Phone (540) 458-8191. E-mail: Brannere@wlu.edu*

> *Structuring part of a major gift as a challenge shows an organization's willingness to pay its own way.*

## 68. Trustees Drive Multimillion-dollar Challenge

Lawrence University (Appleton, WI) recently rolled out a three-year, $3 million challenge in hopes of gaining $6 million. And after the unexpectedly overwhelming success of a six-week blitz fundraiser, the Trustee Triple Treat Challenge (see box, below), organizers have no doubt they will meet that goal, says Stacy Mara, director of annual giving.

"We already had this challenge planned," Mara says, "but this is a collective trustee challenge rather than a challenge aimed at just a few individuals."

The goal of the challenge is to raise $3 million in funds, which will be matched, dollar for dollar, by the trustees who have already pledged $3 million in support over the next three years. Unlike their very successful Trustee Triple Treat Challenge, Mara notes that this fundraiser is also open to parents and friends of the school, as well as alumni.

Hopes were for the new challenge to draw donors who did not give in fiscal year '09 and those donors who have been at the same gifting level for several years, she says: "Our experience has been that once donors reach a certain level, say $100 or $500, they get stuck. The idea here is to encourage them to move up to that next level."

To do so, university staff offered a dollar-for-dollar match to persons who did not give in fiscal year '09. For those who did donate, a match was given when their fiscal year '10 donation allowed them to move to the next giving level.

Donors could sign on to participate over the next three years, giving the university the ability to plan based on promised funds and donors the ability to see their gift doubled.

Advertising began in July with a Q&A article, The Economy, the College, and the Road That Lies Ahead, with Terry Franke, class of 1968 and Bob Anker, class of 1964 (www.lawrence.edu/news/pubs/lt/Summer09/WEB%20PDFs.PDF/024-025.pdf). In August, university staff released an e-mail video appeal to promote the trustee challenge. In September, class agents promoted the event in solicitation letters to classmates.

Further promotion occurred through December and included a reply envelope in the Report on Giving magazine, solicitation letter from President Jill Beck, and a second e-mail video appeal promoting the final days of the campaign in December.

*Source: Stacy J. Mara, Director of Annual Giving, Lawrence University, Appleton, WI. Phone (920) 832-6557. E-mail: stacy.j.mara@lawrence.edu*

Content not available in this edition

### New Twist on Old Challenge Raises Nearly $1 Million in Six Weeks

In late fiscal year 2009, staff at Lawrence University (Appleton, WI) knew they needed a push to reach their funding goal. And so, the Trustee Triple Treat Challenge was born, wrapped in eye-catching pink flyers with a triple-scoop ice cream cone logo; a stretch for a university that is typically very traditional.

Stacy Mara, director of annual giving, says the idea came to her as she looked at trustee pledge commitments for fiscal year '09 and '10: "We were actually planning for a fiscal year '10 challenge and asking our trustees to make five-year Lawrence Fund pledges starting in fiscal year '10. Some of the trustees stepped up in fiscal year '09, so we decided that given our need for a boost... we'd use the fiscal year '09 trustee gifts and put forth the Trustee Triple Treat."

Stacy approached two trustees before presenting her idea to the campaign steering committee, ultimately gaining approval of the challenge at the board of trustees' May meeting.

This challenge promised not just a match of alumni donations, but a double match, effectively tripling any alumni contribution. The result? An astounding $929,027 in funding. The three trustees specifically targeted for the challenge were those that had stepped up in fiscal year '09.

Staff sent alumni an e-mail blast in May explaining the challenge and letting donors know they had through June to take part. They posted the challenge on the school's website and sent a mailing. Mara says the challenge was open specifically to alumni, 1,147 of whom participated for a total of $309,676 in alumni funds. Add that to the $619,351 in matching contributions and Lawrence University raised nearly $1 million in six weeks, exceeding fiscal year '08 donations by 2.5 percent.

## 69. Closing Options

- **Bottom-up method** — Help the prospect to make decisions on matters subordinate to the pledge: type of gift, how it would be used, what the fund might be named, who and how many the gift would benefit and so forth. Decisions on these matters help to visualize the gift and how it will look after it is made.

## 70. Six Key Strategies for Meeting A Once-in-a-lifetime Challenge

What would you do with an all-or-nothing, once-in-a-lifetime opportunity?

Development staff at Trinity College (Hartford, CT) recently faced that question with a challenge to beat all challenges: An anonymous donor promised an immediate $5 million gift if they could achieve a gift participation rate of 55 percent or higher among Trinity's 20,000 living alumni. Failure to do so would mean the college would receive nothing.

In the end, the college achieved a giving rate of 55.34 percent, the highest alumni engagement rate among Connecticut institutions of higher education, and projected to be among the top 10 highest rates among two- and four-year colleges and universities across the country, says Gretchen Orschiedt, director of development.

Helping them accomplish this in just six short months, Orschiedt says, was the fact it was an all-or-nothing opportunity.

"All who volunteered and donated knew that it would be down to the last days that the challenge requirement would be met and that their help was critical," she says. "At Trinity, we do not receive $5 million gifts every day — this was a transformative endowment gift for the college — and all who were involved received this message."

To make sure all potential donors learned of this opportunity, Trinity staff:

1. **Employed extensive use of social media.** Trinity officials posted frequent Facebook messages and Twitter posts, including offering a Facebook Donor Badge to persons who gave online. They also e-mailed persons who made gifts before the challenge was announced, including an e-mail text that they could forward to all of their Trinity friends.
2. **Segmented donors.** This allowed specific individuals (e.g., faculty, coaches) to communicate the challenge message to a specific audience, such as former students or players.
3. **Brought goals to the class level.** Rather than focusing on the larger number needed to reach 55 percent participation, annual fund staff used individual class figures (e.g., "Your class is only 10 gifts away from reaching its goal!") to add emphasis to the need.
4. **Made sure recorded messages stood out.** A high-profile, famous alum and the associate director of athletics provided the unique voices for these calls that went out to remind prospective donors of the urgency of the message in the final weeks of the campaign.
5. **Provided weekly updates to volunteers on progress and need.** Toward the end of the campaign, these updates became daily updates.
6. **Utilized additional resources.** Even volunteers not normally charged with soliciting, such as trustees, took on that role in this campaign. Volunteers received online resources (e.g., a challenge case statement, Q&A and a volunteer to-do list with easy steps for reaching out to alumni about the challenge).

*Source: Gretchen Orschiedt, Director of Development, Trinity College, Hartford, CT. Phone (860) 297-4123. E-mail: gretchen.orschiedt@trincoll.edu*

*The closer you are to the end of your challenge campaign, the more frequent your progress updates should be.*

## 71. How to Pick an Effective Challenge Donor

Most challenge gifts are initiated by the benefiting institution itself, says Ronald Joyce, vice president for college advancement Trinity College (Hartford, CT). The question, then, is what kind of prospects would respond to such an idea.

Joyce, who recently oversaw a campaign that raised alumni donation rates from 47 to 55 percent, and thereby won a $5 million all-or-nothing challenge grant, offers several characteristics to look for in a potential challenge donor:

- **Financial capacity.** "We have all become immune to large numbers, so challenges of $100,000 or $200,000 don't get much attention anymore. You want to identify someone who can give a gift large enough to be meaningful."

- **Competitive streak.** "The best challenge donors are inherently competitive. You want someone who wants to see something about your organization improved, and is willing to put his money where his ambitions are."

- **Uncompromising nature.** Joyce says he is positive the Trinity donor would not have given a single dollar if the participation goal had not been met — and that this was a good thing. "It was a great motivator for the staff, and that urgency filtered down to the volunteers and the donors themselves."

*Source: Ronald Joyce, Vice President for College Advancement, Trinity College, Hartford, CT. Phone (860) 297-2361. E-mail: Ronald.joyce@trincoll.edu*

*Soft challenges often fail to produce as much donor response as firm, do-or-die commitments.*

## 72. $10 Million Challenge Gift To Support Endowed Chairs

In April 2008, Irwin Jacobs, chairman of the Salk Institute for Biological Studies (La Jolla, CA), and his wife, Joan, established a $10 million matching fund to support the creation of 10 senior scientist endowed chairs.

The Irwin and Joan Jacobs Leadership Challenge will match 10 gifts of $2 million with a $1 million gift, providing each chair with a $3 million endowment. Each endowment will be used to create and name a permanent chair at the institute and provide key support to a Salk Institute senior scientist.

"Donors to this challenge can get a bargain on an endowed chair, but they still have to be able to give $2 million, so it has not been an easy task, especially in this market," says Rebecca Newman, vice president of development and communications. "We have so far funded two of the endowed chairs and three other proposals are out."

The idea for the challenge was mutually germinated, says Newman. "Irwin Jacobs understands that the highest priority for Salk is the ability to retain the most senior faculty. The Jacobses have been very helpful in identifying and cultivating those who would be good prospects for an endowed chair."

Newman says they have so far identified 50 prospective donors to the challenge and will most likely have to identify many more to endow all 10 chairs. All prospects are loyal donors with a special interest in the scientific areas the endowed chairs will support. "I expect the challenge will take another year to a year-and-a-half to complete," she says. "All cultivation is one-on-one. Donors get to know the scientists and get to see them at work in the lab."

Stewardship of these challenge donors is personal and frequent, says Newman. "The endowed chairs keep in close contact with their donors. Donors are the first to be informed of breakthroughs in the lab."

The challenge is not part of a capital campaign, she says, but was rather part of a process of identifying critical needs.

*Source: Rebecca Newman, Vice President, Development and Communications, Salk Institute for Biological Studies, La Jolla, CA. Phone (858) 453-4100. E-mail: rnewman@salk.edu*

*Focusing challenges on large-figure gifts can be an effective way of developing new major donors.*

## 73. Participation Challenge Capitalizes On Spirit Week Fever

Spirit week is always a time of great pride and celebration. Use this special period to raise needed revenue and cultivate new supporters.

Show your Spirit through your Gift was the tagline of Episcopal High School's (Alexandria, VA) Roll Call Challenge — a week-long challenge campaign seeking 110 gifts supporting the school's annual fund in honor of its 110th football game against arch-rival Woodberry Forest.

"Spirit week draws lots of younger alumni, and we wanted to capitalize on the enthusiasm that naturally surrounds it," says Elizabeth Woodcock, director of annual giving.

The challenge was publicized through a dedicated spirit week Web page as well as through e-mail, Facebook, Twitter and e-newsletters. Woodcock says an important part of winning the challenge was ensuring that all electronic communications were accompanied by a large "Donate Now" button taking users to an online donation form.

The challenge generated 119 gifts and more than $135,000 in just seven days. The biggest victories, though, were the connections built between alumni and the annual fund, says Woodcock.

"One family had made a pledge for the year, but they increased it just so it would count towards the challenge," she says. "Creating that kind of community buy-in and connection with a cherished tradition is very exciting for us."

*Source: Elizabeth Woodcock, Director of Annual Giving, Episcopal High School, Alexandria, VA. Phone (703) 933-4056. E-mail: Emw@episcopalhighschool.org*

*Synchronizing challenge campaigns with meaningful milestones (anniversaries, celebrations, etc) can increase participation dramatically.*

## 74. Celebrate the Achievement Of Meeting a Donor's Challenge

Never miss the opportunity to celebrate the achievement of meeting a donor's challenge. Involve both the challenge donor and those who joined in matching the challenge.

Think outside the box to make your challenge achievement celebration a special experience for everyone who attends. Here's a sampling of ideas you may wish to incorporate:

✓ Have a ceremonial tree planting to signify the long-term impact of this project on your organization and those you serve. Name the tree in honor of the challenger.

✓ Line up a surprise appearance by someone who is special in the life of the challenge donor: a family member or members, an old friend, a former colleague or a celebrity.

✓ Have two or three people who will benefit from the impact of the gifts — students, youth — offer words of appreciation to the challenge donor and everyone who rose to the challenge.

✓ Depending on the size of your donor pool, take the time to announce the name of everyone who financially supported the project.

✓ Unveil an attractive donor wall that displays the names of everyone who supported the project.

Celebrating the successful completion of a challenge gift adds meaning to the reason for giving. It tells everyone, "Together we made this happen!"

*Celebrating the completion of a challenge not only recognizes the donor, it encourages others to make challenges of their own.*

## 75. Imagine the Possibilities That Exist

Before approaching an individual or a business for a challenge gift, spend some time thinking about and brainstorming all of the possibilities that might exist. That up front planning may lead to new opportunities you had not previously considered.

Review this Q&A sampling as a way to begin thinking about the many challenge gift possibilities that exist:

*What different factors can come into play when considering challenge gift possibilities?*

Several criteria: The intent behind the challenge (e.g. to motivate board giving, to motivate new and increased giving, to encourage planned gifts), the challenge amount, duration of the challenge, who the challenge is aimed at, the challenge-to-match ratio, how the challenger's gift will be used, how donors' matching gifts will be used and more.

*What if I contact several prospects asking them to establish a challenge gift and more than one of them agrees to my invitation?*

Nice problem. Ask them each to join in a collaborative challenge. Instead of publicizing a 1:1 match, you may be able to offer a 2:1 or a 3:1 match depending on the number of challenge participants.

*Is it possible to have more than one challenge going on at the same time?*

Absolutely, as long as each supports a different purpose. You might have one challenge in place directed to your entire mailing list that's aimed at increasing support for your annual fund and another, more narrow in scope, that challenges major donors to make a gift to your endowment fund.

*How do we identify who we should go after for a challenge gift?*

Those who have a past history of supporting your organization in a big way would make the most obvious choices. However, the publicity surrounding a challenge gift might be what it takes to motivate a non-donor to rise to the occasion. As you develop a list of likely candidates — individuals, businesses, foundations — prepare a list of benefits for each. The personalized benefits you identify for each prospect may help you to prioritize who should be called on first, second and so forth.

*What sorts of benefits might you identify for a challenge prospect?*

Although some benefits will obviously be universal for any prospect, others might be more tailored to that prospect's wants and needs. The benefits you list for a financial institution prospect would obviously be different than those you would list for an individual prospect. The benefits would also be influenced by the amount and type of publicity that surrounds the challenge.

*Would it be wise to have a challenge gift agreement prepared, reviewed and signed by both parties (challenge donor and your organization)?*

Without a doubt. The signed agreement, not unlike many major gift agreements, should spell out all of the details that both parties have agreed to, including whether receipt of the challenge gift is contingent upon fully meeting the criteria set forth.

Challenge gifts are one of the most publicity-friendly forms of donation. Use this fact when seeking challenge donors.

## 76. Inter-college Participation Challenge Motivates Young Alumni

Many educational institutions find it difficult to involve "GOLD" alumni — graduates of the last decade — in annual funding needs. Officials at four liberal arts colleges in the northeast found they could tackle the problem better together than alone.

March Mania, the challenge they developed in collaboration, pitted GOLD alumni from Hamilton, Bates, Trinity and Colby in a race to secure the most annual commitments and lay claim to the title of most loyal alumni.

"The idea was to provide a firm deadline and an incentive to encourage young alumni giving," says Jon Hysell, executive director of alumni relations and annual giving at Hamilton (Clinton, NY). "The competition between peer institutions encouraged participation, but in the end, everyone won."

The contest began with a meeting to formulate ground rules. "It's important to establish a mutually-acceptable definition of what an annual gift is," says Hysell. "Is a gift from an alumni couple one gift or two? Is a gift in honor of five friends one gift or five? Everyone needs to be on the same page."

Once that groundwork was in place, a shared website was established and a common reporting format developed. Advancement officers kept in frequent contact during the contest, speaking regularly on the phone and exchanging donation updates via Googledocs (docs.google.com).

Collaboration was not limited to back-end logistics, however. Volunteers from the four colleges twice gathered for shared phone-a-thons. Three post-challenge parties also provided an opportunity to celebrate shared victories.

Hamilton, which finished second in the contest, received 661 gifts (including 123 on the final day) and exceeded 50 percent GOLD participation for the first time in 11 years. Similar increases were seen among the other colleges, with Bates receiving the most monthly GOLD donations in its history.

Just as important, though, were the channels of collaboration established between the schools, says Hysell. "Being able to collaborate on this and other projects is a source of real professional value for our development officers. It's something we can all use going forward."

*Source: Jon Hysell, Executive Director of Alumni Relations and Annual Giving, Hamilton College, Clinton, NY. Phone (315) 859-4606. E-mail: jahysell@hamilton.edu*

*Competition between donor groups (class years in an alumni body, departments in an organization) can be a great way of stimulating support.*

Lightning Source UK Ltd.
Milton Keynes UK
UKOW01f0754060813

214894UK00007B/355/P